The Best Lunchbo

Variety is the spice of life and that includes lunchtime and the lunchbox. Plan a different lunch for every day.

Variety is also the key to a healthy, balanced diet. Try not to pack the same old sandwich, packet of crisps (potato chips), and piece of fruit every day. Besides not providing children with the variety they need, it also becomes dull and may well arrive back at home uneaten.

It is important that children eat lunch so that their concentration levels are maintained during the afternoon. There is evidence that what your children eat affects their behavior after a meal, so it has never been more important to ensure you pack a good lunchbox. Minerals and vitamins found in fruit and vegetables will provide vital elements for good health and will help your children do to their best at school.

Bite-size foods

Instead of sandwiches, why not give a younger child a selection of bite-size foods to nibble on. Cubes of cheese, slices of ham, mini sausages, hard boiled eggs, sticks of carrot and celery, and cherry tomatoes can be packed into small containers. You can also supply small containers of dips such as hummus to serve with the vegetable sticks, along with a few corn chips to create a nutritious, balanced meal.

Pasta salad

Add some variety by packing a pasta salad in the lunchbox. You can make a simple one by mixing cooked pasta with cubes of cheese or ham, diced pepper, and halved cherry tomatoes, then tossing in a little mayonnaise.

Rice salad

Another type of salad that is sure to please is a rice salad. Mix cooked rice with diced peppers and cucumber, and with cooked peas and diced carrots (let the cooked vegetables cool down before adding them to the salad). Toss in a little vinaigrette dressing.

Bread and cake

Remember your child needs a lot of energy to keep going through the day, so include some carbohydrates. This may be bread, but it can also be supplied as a muffin (see pages 14-15), piece of cake, or a biscuit (cookie) - as long as it isn't too sweet.

Fruit

Include some fruit for vital nutrients. This may be a single piece of fruit or a mini fruit salad. Dried fruits such as apricots, prunes, apple slices, and sultanas are good to include for healthy nibbles.

Or make your own fruit yogurt - it will have much less sugar than those bought from the shops. Stir chopped fruit into natural (plain) yogurt and sweeten with a little honey. If your child doesn't like chunks, purée soft fruits such as strawberries, blueberries, or raspberries in a blender and stir into the yogurt.

Quick Tip
Don't forget to include a drink in the lunchbox. Water is best, but you can also pack diluted fruit juice as a healthy option.

 Variation Replace the lettuce leaves with other healthy green options such as **spinach** or **rocket** (arugula).

Chicken Club Sandwich

These hearty sandwiches are ideal for the lunchbox, but if eating at home, you can also add slices of tomato.

Serves 2
15 minutes

Ingredients

4 rashers (slices) bacon

6 thin slices of crusty bread

Mayonnaise

175g/6oz cooked chicken, sliced

2 tbsp mayonnaise (optional)

Few salad leaves or watercress

1 tomato, sliced

Smart Shopper

The peppery dark green leaves of watercress are among the most nutritious salad greens. When buying watercress, look for crisp, bright green leaves, avoiding those that are wilted or yellow. If the flavor is too strong for your children, use the milder lettuce leaves instead.

① Grill or fry the bacon until crispy.

① Toast the bread if desired. Spread two slices of bread with a little mayonnaise.

② Top two slices of bread with the chicken, then with mayonnaise and some lettuce leaves or watercress.

③ Place a slice of bread on top of the chicken and spread with a little mayonnaise.

④ Place the bacon and tomato on the bread and sandwich together with the remaining bread.

⑤ Cut the two sandwiches in half or quarters and serve.

Quick Tip
If you use thicker bread, make each sandwich with only 2 slices of bread, omitting the middle slice of bread.

 Variation Add some chopped **black olives** instead of the celery and onion and top with a slice of **avocado** after melting the cheese.

Tuna Melt

This is a quick, nutritious lunch that can be made in minutes.

 Serves 2
15 minutes

Ingredients

200g/7oz can tuna, drained

6 spring onions (scallions), sliced

1 stick celery, thinly sliced

½ red bell pepper, diced

6 tbsp mayonnaise

4 slices bread

Few leaves of lettuce (optional)

2 slices of cheese

Smart Shopper

Get cheesy by choosing the right cheese to go with the tuna melt. Kids often object to strong flavors, so use a mild cheese to make this one a hit with your kids. For a more adult taste, try a strong aged cheddar. A little will go a long way, so you can get a great cheese taste with a smaller quantity of strong cheese, which cuts down on fat.

① Mix together the tuna, onions, celery, pepper, and mayonnaise until well combined.

② Lightly toast the bread under a hot grill (broiler).

③ Place the lettuce, if using, on two slices of toast, and divide the tuna mixture between the two.

④ Place a slice of cheese on top and return to the grill (broiler). Heat until the cheese melts.

⑤ Top with the remaining toast, then cut in half and serve.

Quick Tip
To avoid a runny mixture, squeeze all the liquid from the tuna. After opening the can, push down on the lid, avoiding the sharp edges.

 Variation Try topping the filling with a little grated **Monterey Jack cheese.**

Chicken Fajitas

This Mexican favorite is easy to cook and assemble and should be a hit with the kids.

Serves 2
20 minutes, plus marinating time

Ingredients

2 skinned and boned chicken breasts, about 175g/6oz each

Juice of 2 limes

2 tbsp freshly chopped coriander (cilantro)

2 tbsp sunflower oil

½ tsp chilli flakes

¼ tsp ground coriander

1 each red and green bell pepper, seeded and cut into strips

1 onion, sliced

8 Mexican flour tortillas

Guacamole, tomato salsa, and soured cream

Smart Shopper

Tortillas are flat unleavened bread made from maize (corn) or wheat flour. Corn tortillas have a stronger flavor that is more suitable for beef-based dishes.

Besides using tortillas for Mexican meals, use them wrapped around traditional sandwich fillers such as ham, cheese, and tomato, with a sprinkling of salad dressing.

① Cut the chicken breasts into thin strips and place in a shallow non-metallic dish.

② Combine the lime juice, fresh coriander (cilantro), 1 tbsp oil, chilli, and ground coriander, and pour over the meat. Toss to combine and allow to marinate for at least 30 minutes in the refrigerator.

③ Heat the remaining oil in a frying pan. Remove the chicken from the marinade and add to the pan. Fry over a high heat for about 5 minutes until well browned on all sides.

④ Add the peppers and onion, and fry for 5 minutes until softened. Pour in any remaining marinade and fry for 1 minute.

⑤ Meanwhile, warm the tortillas as directed on the packet.

⑥ Serve filled with the meat mixture, and include a spoonful each of the salsa, guacamole, and soured cream on the side.

Quick Tip

If the chicken breasts still have skin, simply peel it away with your fingers. It's easy to remove flesh from the bone with a sharp knife.

Jacket Potatoes

This versatile dish can be served with butter as a side dish for a main meal or with a choice of fillings for lunch.

Serves 4
1 hour 20 minutes

Ingredients
4 baking potatoes, about 300g/10oz each
Filling of your choice (see below) or butter to serve

Smart Shopper
Not all potatoes are suitable as baking potatoes. Those used for baking are low in moisture and have dry fluffy flesh when cooked. Choose potatoes that are firm with tight skin. Avoid those that have dark spots, cuts, or cracks, and also if they have any signs of green – these will be bitter and can even be poisonous.

① Preheat the oven to 200°C/400°F/gas mark 6. Scrub the potatoes well and prick all over with a fork (to prevent them from exploding in the oven).

② Place on a baking sheet and bake in the hottest part of the oven for 1¼ hours, turning once.

③ When cooked, cut a large cross into the potatoes and squeeze to open out.

④ Place on a serving plate and served topped with a generous wedge of butter or a filling of your choice.

Fillings:

☒ **Baked Beans:** Pour a 400g/14oz can baked beans into a small saucepan and heat gently, stirring, for 4-5 minutes until piping hot.

☒ **Cheese:** Coarsely grate 175g/6oz/1½ cups of cheese and divide between the 4 potatoes.

☒ **Coleslaw:** Allow 50g/2oz/⅓ cup of coleslaw per person.

☒ **Peanut Butter:** Top the potatoes with 2 tbsp of smooth or crunchy peanut butter in place of butter.

☒ **Tuna Mayo:** Mix a 200g/7oz can tuna, drained, with 4 tbsp mayonnaise and 2 tbsp sweet corn niblets (corn kernels).

Quick Tip
A lot of a potato's vitamin content is In the peel, so encourage your children to eat the peel for the most nutritous meal.

 Variation You can add 250g/9oz/2 cups peeled and cubed **squash** or a peeled and chopped **sweet potato** with the leek and carrot.

Easy Vegetable Soup

The combination of vegetables makes this a nutritious lunch, and it is also easy to prepare.

 Serves 4
45 minutes

Ingredients

2 tbsp olive oil

1 leek, sliced

1 clove garlic, chopped

1 carrot, diced

400g/14oz can chopped tomatoes

900ml/30floz/4 cups vegetable stock

1 courgette (zucchini), diced

1 red bell pepper, seeded and diced

50g/2oz short-cut macaroni

Salt and freshly ground black pepper

4 tsp pesto or basil leaves to garnish

Grated fresh Parmesan cheese to sprinkle

Smart Shopper

You can use a store-bought vegetable stock but they are not as good as homemade. To make your own, simmer 1 sliced onion, leek, carrot, and parsnip, plus 6 cloves of crushed garlic, with 1400ml/48floz/6 cups of water and some dried herbs of your choice for 45 to 60 minutes. Strain the stock through a sieve.

1. Heat the oil in a large saucepan, add the leek and carrot, and gently fry for 5 minutes until the vegetables begin to soften. Do not let them burn.

2. Stir in the garlic and fry for 1 minute.

3. Stir in the tomatoes and stock, and bring to the boil. Simmer for 20 minutes.

4. Add the courgette (zucchini), red pepper, and macaroni, and simmer for 10 minutes. Season with salt and pepper.

5. Serve in warm bowls with a spoonful of pesto or a few basil leaves and sprinkle with Parmasan cheese.

Quick Tip
Trimming the ends of the clove of garlic with a sharp knife will make it easier to remove the skin before you chop the garlic.

 Variation You can add some freshly grated **Parmesan cheese** if you like. Sprinkle it over the butter.

Garlic Bread

This is a great accompaniment to soup, salad, and pasta, all of which are ideal for lunch.

 Serves 4
30 minutes

2 cloves garlic, crushed

1 tbsp freshly chopped parsley

115g/4oz/1 stick butter, softened

1 loaf French bread

Smart Shopper

Fresh crusty bread is the most important ingredient in this recipe. If you can't find fresh French bread, then try a different type of crusty bread or even rolls. Bread from the supermarket may contain preservatives, so try purchasing bread from a local bakery.

1. Preheat the oven to 180°C/350°F/gas mark 4.
2. Place the garlic, parsley, and butter in a mixing bowl, and beat with a wooden spoon until well combined.
3. Cut the bread into 2.5-cm/1-inch thick slices.
4. Spread each slice with the seasoned butter and reassemble the loaf.
5. Wrap the loaf well in foil. It may be easier to do this in two parcels.
6. Bake for 20 minutes. Serve while still hot.

Quick Tip
Cut the bread all the way through so you can separate the hot slices easily when served, but reassemble in a loaf shape before you bake it.

 Variation For an interesting change, try adding a little diced **red pepper**.

Guacamole with Chips

This makes a nice snack on its own, or serve with Chicken Fajitas (see pages 8-9) to make a Mexican dinner.

 Serves 4
30 minutes

Ingredients

2 ripe avocados

2 tbsp lemon juice

2 tomatoes

½ small onion, finely chopped

1 clove garlic, crushed

½ tsp ground cumin

½ tsp ground coriander

2 tbsp freshly chopped coriander (cilantro)

Pinch sugar, salt, and freshly ground black pepper

Corn chips to serve

Smart Shopper

Avocados have a bitter taste if cooked, so always use them raw. To tell if an avocado is ripe, squeeze it gently. It should feel tender. If you buy an unripe avocado, it should mature within about 3 days. You can put one in a brown paper bag with an apple to speed up the ripening process. Overripe avocados are only good for using mashed.

① Cut the avocados in half and remove the stone by tapping sharply with the blade of a sharp knife so that it goes into the stone. Twist the knife to remove the stone.

② Scoop out the flesh into a bowl. Add the lemon juice and mash coarsely with a fork.

③ Skin the tomatoes if desired. Cut in half, then scoop out and discard the seeds. Chop the flesh.

④ Add the tomato, onion, garlic, ground cumin and coriander, and chopped coriander (cilantro) to the bowl, and beat to combine.

⑤ Season with the sugar, salt, and pepper.

⑥ Transfer to a serving dish and serve with the corn chips.

Quick Tip
To peel a tomato, put it in boiling water for 1 minute, then cold water for 1 minute. Cut into the skin with a knife, then use fingers to peel it off.

 Variation Instead of lettuce on one half of a bun, replace with a slice of your favorite **cheese** and melt under the grill (broiler) for a minute or so.

Hamburgers

Named after Hamburg in Germany, hamburgers are made with beef. Tasty homemade burgers are easy to make.

 Serves 4
30 minutes

Ingredients

700g/1lb8oz minced (ground) beef

Salt and freshly ground black pepper

1 tsp chilli powder or dried mixed herbs

4 burger buns

Handful of salad leaves

2 tomatoes, sliced

Sliced pickles

Smart Shopper
When choosing your minced (ground) beef, look for meat that has some fat to help the cooking process but not so much fat (the meat will have a pale pink color) that it all shrinks away. Look for pale red or pink meat; red means additives. Untreated beef naturally darkens when exposed to light – this is fine. Make sure it has a fresh smell.

① Place the beef in a large mixing bowl and season well with salt and pepper. Sprinkle the chilli powder or herbs over the meat, and using your fingers, mix until well combined.

② Press the meat together and shape into 4 burgers, no more than 2.5cm/1 inch thick. Cook the burgers under a medium-hot grill for 5-6 minutes each side or until cooked through.

③ Cut the burger buns in half and lightly toast if desired. Place one half on each serving plate and place a few salad leaves on each. Place a burger on the salad leaves and top with sliced tomatoes and pickles.

④ Place the burger bun on top and serve immediately.

Quick Tip
To shape a burger "patty", form a ball of the meat. Press the ball between the palm of your hands and rotate it to form an even round circle.

 Variation Rice (see pages 70-71) is an ideal accompaniment for this dish.

Chicken Satay Kebabs

This is a fun way to serve chicken, but make sure there are no peanut allergies in the family before serving to younger children.

 Serves 4
20 minutes, plus marinating time

Ingredients

2 chicken breasts, skinned and boned

4 tbsp sunflower oil

2 cloves garlic, crushed

1 tsp caster (superfine) sugar

½ tsp ground cumin

½ tsp ground coriander

1 tbsp light soy sauce

Satay sauce:

8 tbsp smooth peanut butter

8 tbsp hot chicken stock

½ tsp chilli powder

Smart Shopper

The Chinese and Japanese use soy sauce in their cuisine. The Chinese make dark and light soy sauce, with the dark sauce being fermented longer and having a stronger taste, more suitable for adults. The standard Japanese soy sauce (sometimes labelled shoyu) is light compared to Chinese soy sauce. It is also sweeter and less salty.

① Cut each chicken breast lengthways into 8 long strips. Combine the oil, garlic, sugar, spices, and soy sauce in a shallow dish and add the chicken strips. Toss to coat the strips and let marinate for at least 1 hour, up to 12 hours, in the refrigerator.

② Thread the chicken strips onto skewers and cook under a hot grill (broiler) for 6-8 minutes, turning frequently.

③ While the chicken is cooking, combine the peanut butter, stock, and chilli powder to form a smooth sauce.

④ Serve the chicken strips still on the skewers with the peanut sauce.

Quick Tip

If you use wooden skewers, first soak them in a bowl of cold water for 30 minutes to prevent them from burning under the grill.

 Variation Experiment with the combination of vegetables – try adding sliced **mushrooms**, diced **red pepper**, and **broccoli** florets.